# DOGS & DOGS!

Photographs by Araldo De Luca

WHITE STAR PUBLISHERS

Editorial Project: Valeria Manferto De Fabianis   -   Graphic Design: Clara Zanotti

Preface and Text: Caterina Gromis di Trana   -   Editorial Assistant: Giorgio Ferrero

# DOGS & DOGS!

## Photographs by Araldo De Luca

"The dogs portrayed in this volume have all been bred by Italian dogs' breeders
of high quality which regularly attend dogs' shows and training sessions.
The breeders strictly follow the rules and the standards established by E.N.C.I.
(*Ente Nazionale della Cinofilia Italiana*, National Authority for Italian Love of Dogs).
The specimen born before 2004 respect the aesthetic rules required
at the time they were born.
Whatever else interpretation of these pictures has to be seen as arbitrary
and against what is agreed by the current E.N.C.I. regulations."

"Ranzham," Clumber Spaniel

"Martino," Weimaraner

"Ramiro," German Shepherd

"Bannerun Dreamscape," English Setter

# CONTENTS

Preface by
CATERINA GROMIS DI TRANA

Yes, it's them, the descendants of wolves. We know some of them still feature traces of the ancient past in their look and behavior. Even Dachshunds? Pekinese? Chihuahuas? Yes, the wild progenitor is the same for all, Cockers and Mastiffs, Great Danes and Pugs, and even though our wit modified their shape according to our fashions, customs and whims, dogs should be treated like wolves. Skillful survivors, they managed to carve out an ingenious survival strategy outside the predator world from which they hail, putting to good use their extremely sophisticated social behavior. They put their sympathy to our service, those amazing biological freeloaders.

# The thousand faces of dogs:

## a fascinating voyage in the dog world

And that's why we should beware: behind those cartoon looks that man chose according to his whims, lie hidden wolves, dogs motivated by canine impulses, canine learning systems, canine perceptions, canine instincts. With humans they share a common feeling, friendship, affection and sometimes heroism, as long as humans are capable of translating their language and acting accordingly. All you need to do is think like a dog. Identify: do not anthropomorphize. That is, it is essential not to make dogs into humans, but act as a dog among dogs. But beware: you must follow the ancient rules of wolves and immediately show them who's the boss. The owner is the leader of the pack. And that's not enough, the owner has to maintain the rank throughout time: any weakness is registered and used at his own expense. History is full of dogs chewing shoes, books, newspapers, carpets, tables, clothes. Not to mention the ones that steal, dig, hump, soil, yelp, woof and howl. Or bite. It's our fault and only ours. Whoever thinks that dogs know they are wrong when they steal a ham from a dinner table, is naïve. Certain owners scold their pup for some misbehavior committed hours before, thinking that the dog will remember and make the connection between the punishment and the act.

Dogs have no sense of morality, they have no feelings of guilt, only the immediate action-reaction connection. If scolded without understanding why, all it can do is persevere and learn to fear its owner, with all the practical and psychological consequences of the case.

The authority of the leader of the pack depends on the balance of little gestures: resolve and affection, compliments and demands. It is amazing to discover how easy it is to obtain obedience with reward rather than with punishment. Authority not arrogance: learning to communicate the right way is a reciprocal joy made of repeated action, reassurances, glances and attention.

Droopy ears, wrinkly face, skin hanging from the lips and neck, sad eyes, are all excuses, fabrications. The diabolical human race selected canine races and copied those "childlike features," well-known by etiologists, which stimulate the instinct to protect their young in all animals. These features that inspire tenderness, are used to highlight personal taste with dogs, individualism. How many times have you seen owner and dog that look alike: some have Schnauzer faces, some German Shepherd, some Jack Russell Terriers and some just look like ordinary dogs. It's a matter of temperament and personal affinity.

In the eyes of a dog people can find ancient human worlds, that speak of hunting and shepherds, caves and stilt-houses, and in the harmony of non-verbal language, people can rediscover emotions that are both familiar and unknown, taken from the microcosm of molecules that miraculously encode our nature.

FINE ART
PORTRAITS

*"Soffcina" and "Martino," Soft-Coated Wheaten Terrier and Weimaraner*

# Face to face with . . .
## all sorts of dogs

You need a lot of patience to make a model out of a dog. In front of the camera, it will lower its head, it will flatten its ears, it will stick its tongue out 6 inches and put on the dumbest expression in the world. And, lo and behold! – it will turn into the magnificent and dignified dog that it really is, just as soon as the camera's back in the bag. . . .

Winds of war

"Miracle." Bulldog

"Clay." Bulldog

Greek profile

"Oro Saiwa," Soft Coated Wheaten Terrier

If you look at a dog
and don't immediately feel love,
you must be a cat

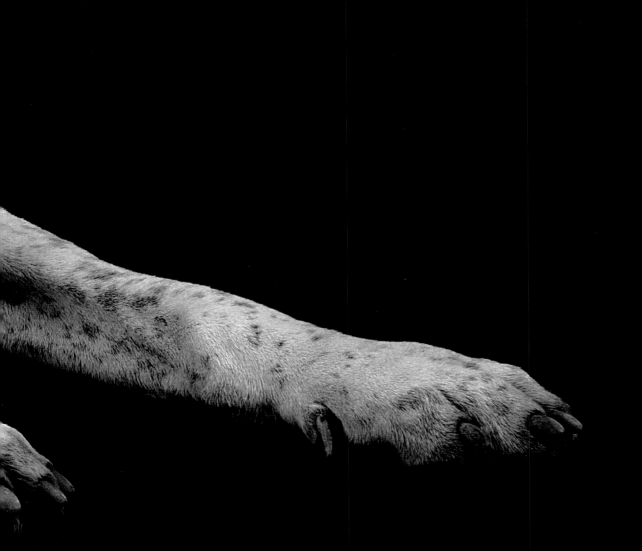

"Luciano." Bracco Italiano

BLUE BLOOD

"Look into a dog's eyes
and try saying that
the animal has no soul"
(Victor Hugo)

"Diamond Dust." Sealyham Terrier

Beard and moustache

*"Diamond Dust," Sealyham Terrier*

CYRANO

*"Prince," Dachshund*

"A dog is a smile and a wagging tail.
What is in between doesn't matter"
(Clara Ortega)

"Primula," Wire-haired Dachshund

Loyalty in one look

BLACK & WHITE

"Dogs possess Beauty without Vanity,
Strength without Insolence,
Courage without Ferocity,
and all the Virtues
of Man without his Vices"

(Lord Byron)

*"Asso," Dalmatian*

KNOWING LOOKS

" Whoever has never kept a
dog does not know what it is
to love and to be loved "
(Arthur Schopenhauer)

*"Ramiro," German Shepherd*

Born to be our friend

"Gaia." German Shepherd

"Niwak." Briard

heration Hippy

"Alban." Briard

48
-
49

HAUTE COIFFURE

*"Rhapsody in Blue," Briard*

ROCK STAR

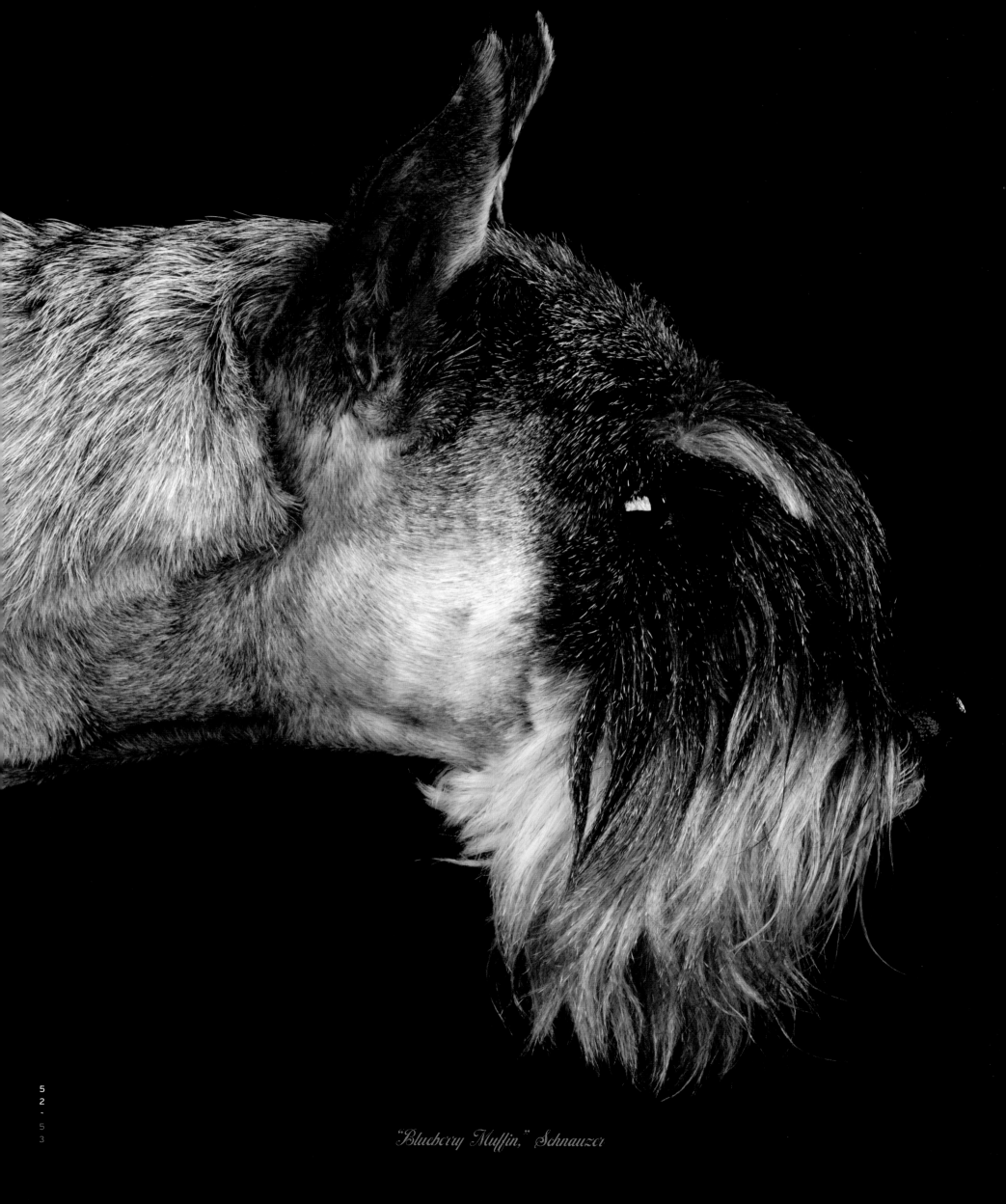

"Blueberry Muffin," Schnauzer

Challenging stares

" Dogs are not our whole life,
but they make our lives whole ""
(Roger Caras)

The unbearable lightness of being

*"Ranzham," Clumber Spaniel*

*"Luna," Bergamasco Sheepdog*

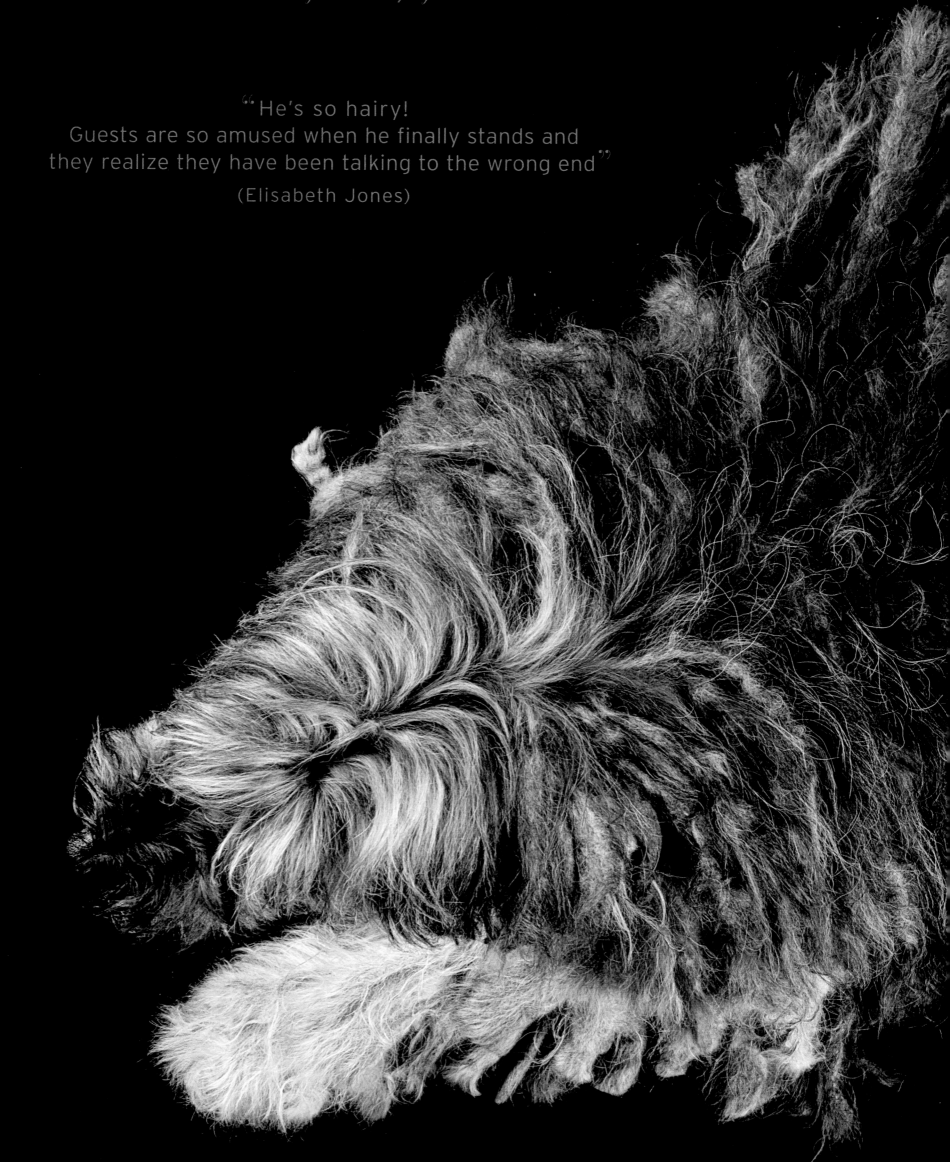

"He's so hairy!
Guests are so amused when he finally stands and
they realize they have been talking to the wrong end"
(Elisabeth Jones)

*"Martine," Weimaraner*

ROYAL PROFILE

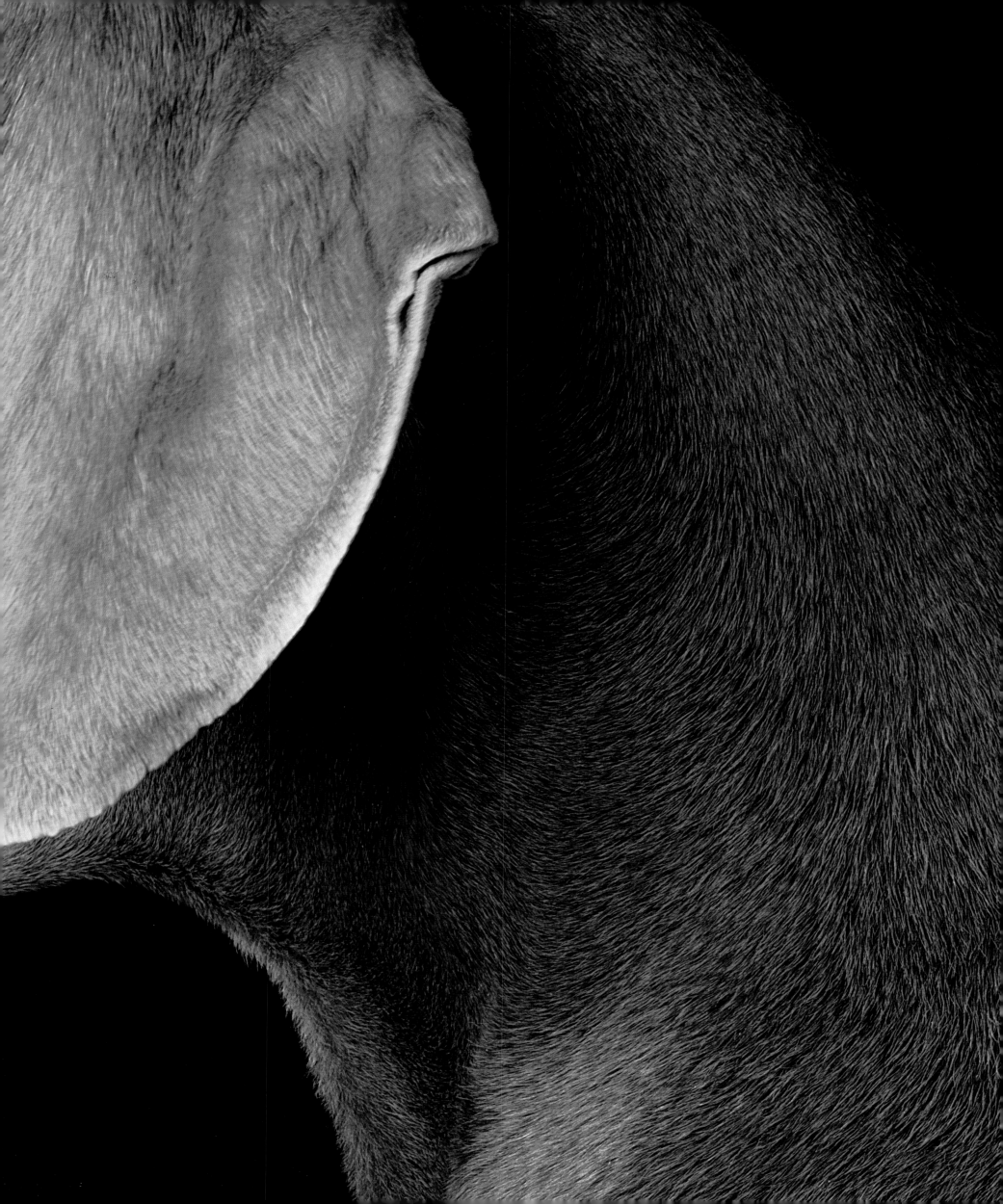

*"Martino," Weimaraner*

"Charlene" and "Angelica," Shar-Pei dogs

A GENTLEMAN DOG

Four-legged aristocracy

"Resolute," Gordon Setters

On . . .

. . . off

*"Sunshine of my Life"* and *"Cochise,"*
*Chow Chows*

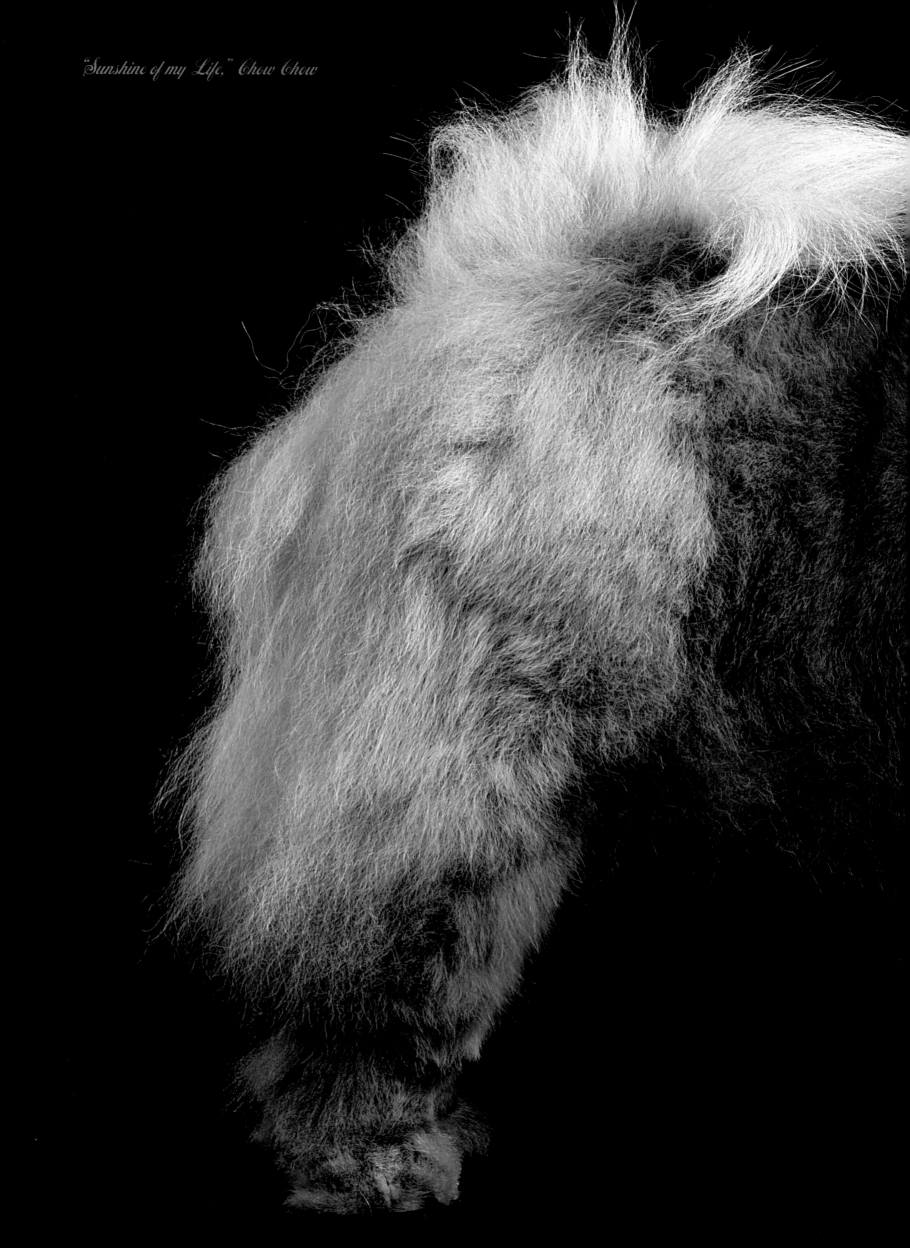

"A barking dog is often more useful than a sleeping lion"
(Washington Irving)

"Game Over." Black Russian Terrier

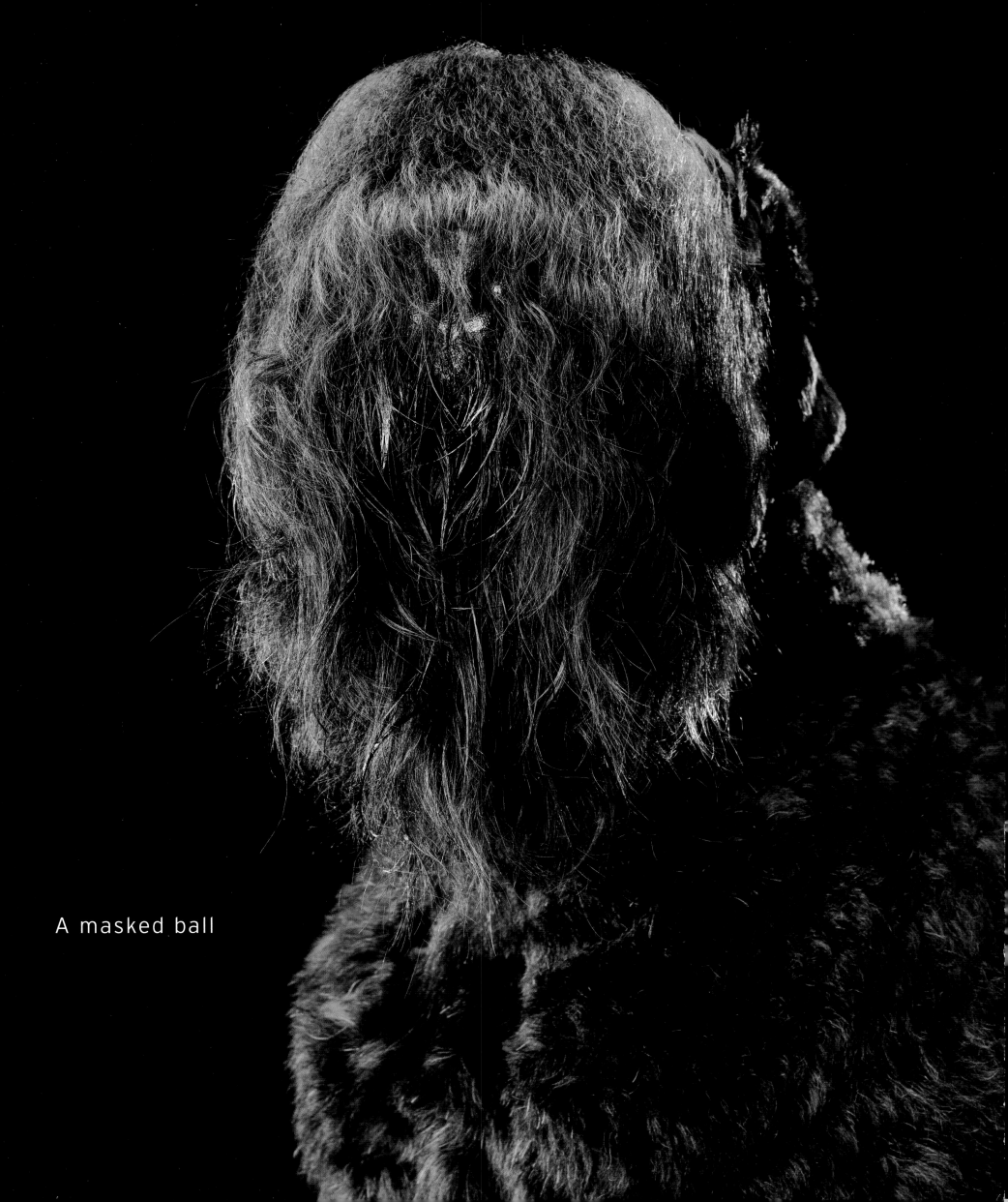

A masked ball

Short legs, high head

"Don Peppe i'uapp." Basset Hound

"A dog has
a philosopher's soul"
(Plato)

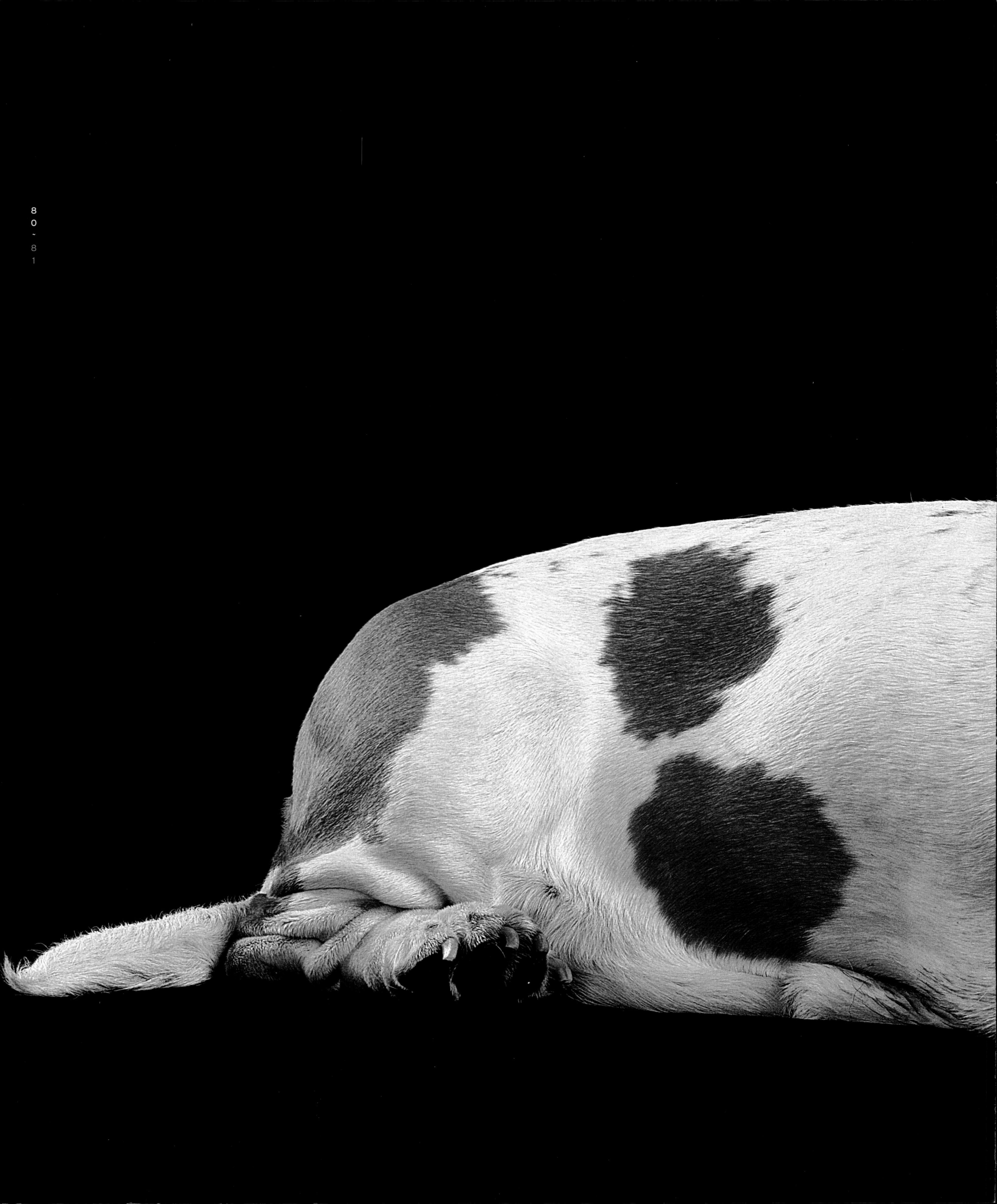

DEAD CALM

LIFE CHANGE

TOTAL BLACK

"Upside Down." Scottish Terrier

"Upside Down," Scottish Terrier

CAFÉ-LATTE

"Malindi." Basenji

"Fall from a Star," Pembroke Welsh Corgi

" There is nothing more precious
than the golden shine of a dog's hair,
shinier than its black eyes,
more unique than its love "
(Enrica Boiocchi)

"Dogs and children are necessary
to the country's well-being as much as
Wall Street and the railway"
(Harry S. Truman)

*"Zoch Serwaj," Airedale Terrier*

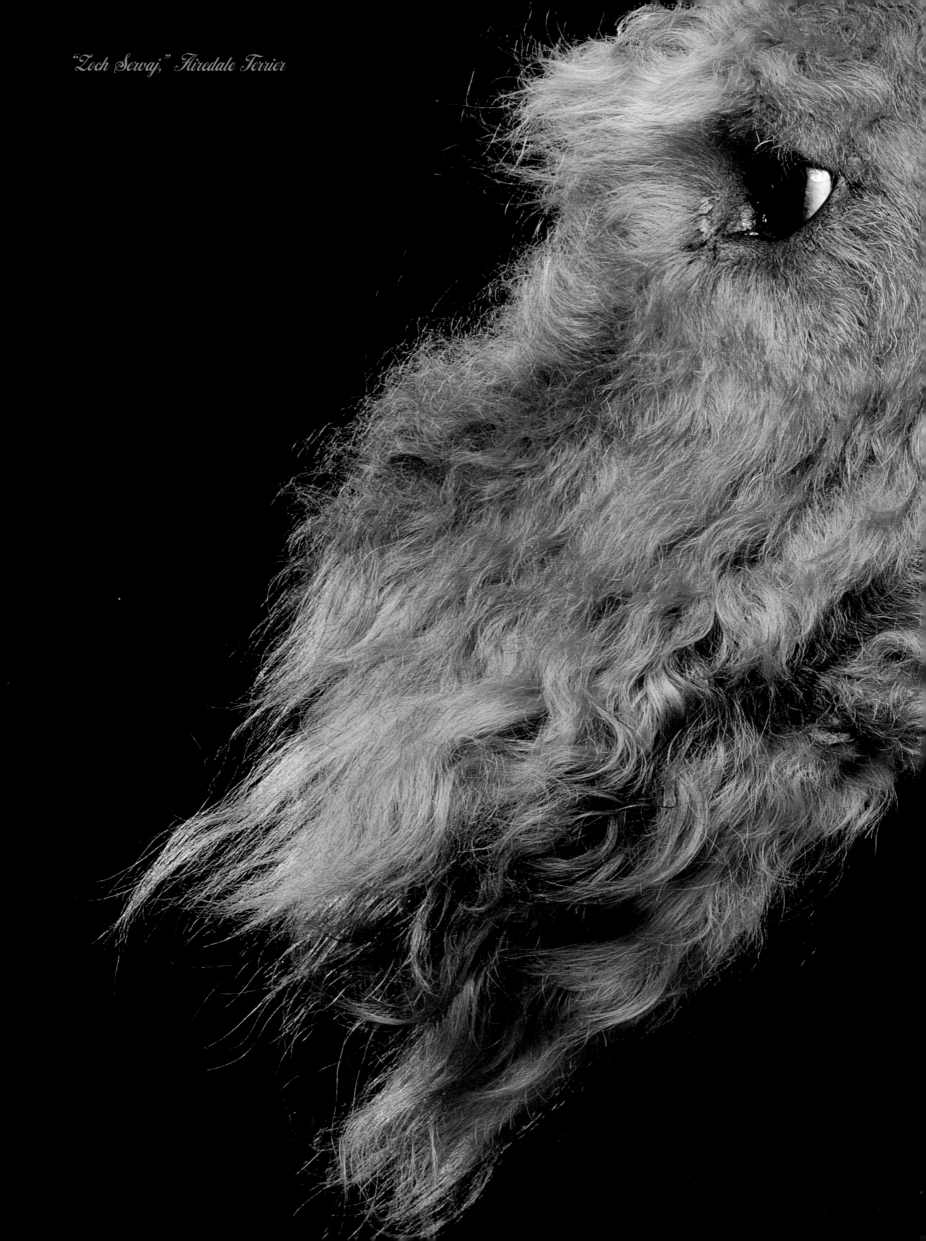

"Zoch Serwaj," Airedale Terrier

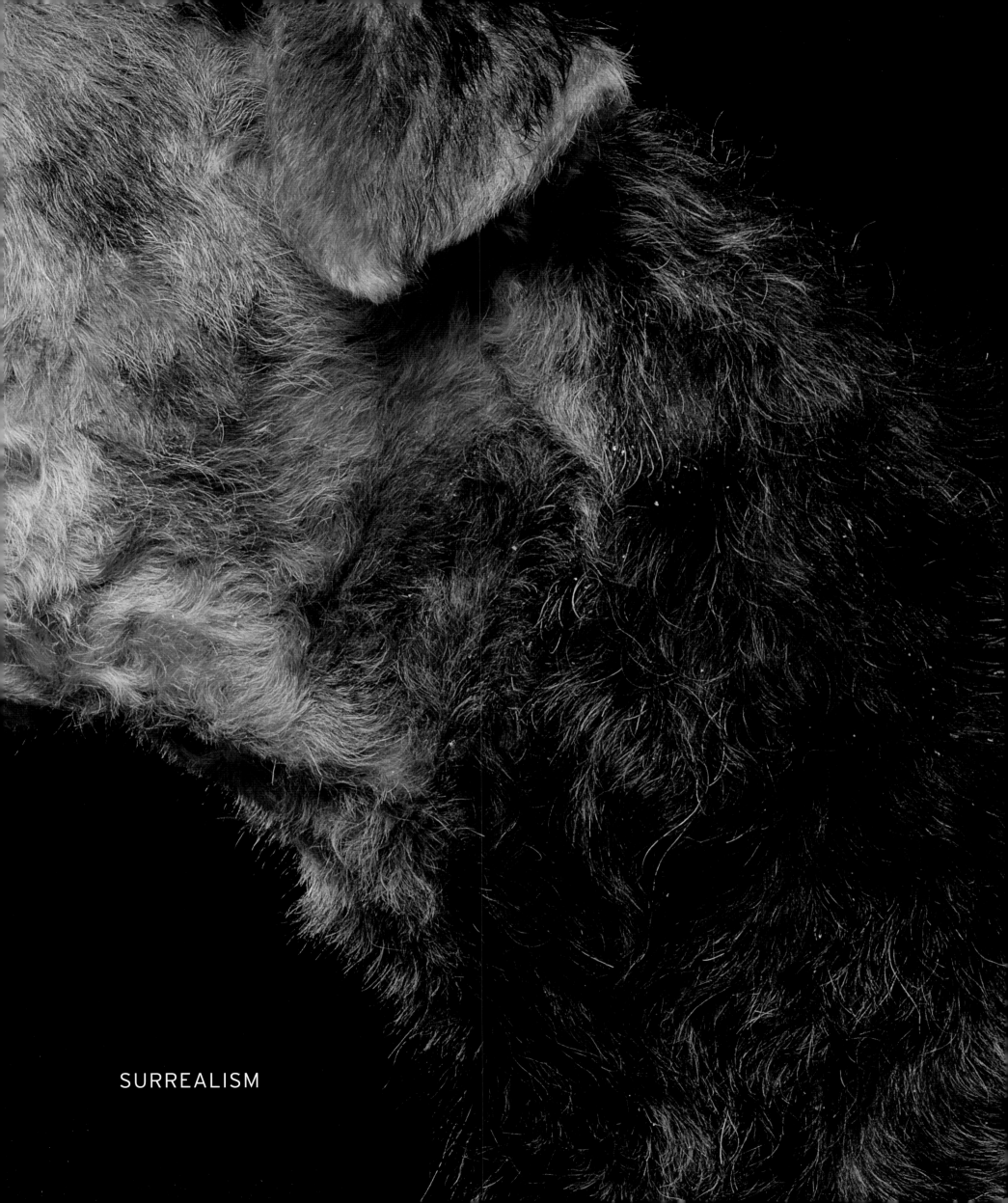

SURREALISM

"Caredig Iowa." Irish Wolfhound

CERBERUS

" A dog is the only thing on this earth
that loves you more than it loves itself "
(Laurence Lindsay)

PHOTO SET

Mischief and . . .

"Misty," Irish Setter

feelings of guilt

*"Bannerun Dreamscape," English Setter*

A matter of style

"Humankind is drawn to dogs
because they are so like ourselves –
bumbling, affectionate, easily disappointed,
fun-loving, grateful for kindness
and the least attention"

(Pam Brown)

"Il Chel Famos," Terranova

"If I weren't a man I would want to be a dog"
(Alexander the Great)

"To lead a dog's life, – people say crying –
but why? . . .
you do exactly what you want every day;
sleep before and after every meal.
People should know!"

(A. P. Herbert)

"Ustica." Boxer

Deep thoughts

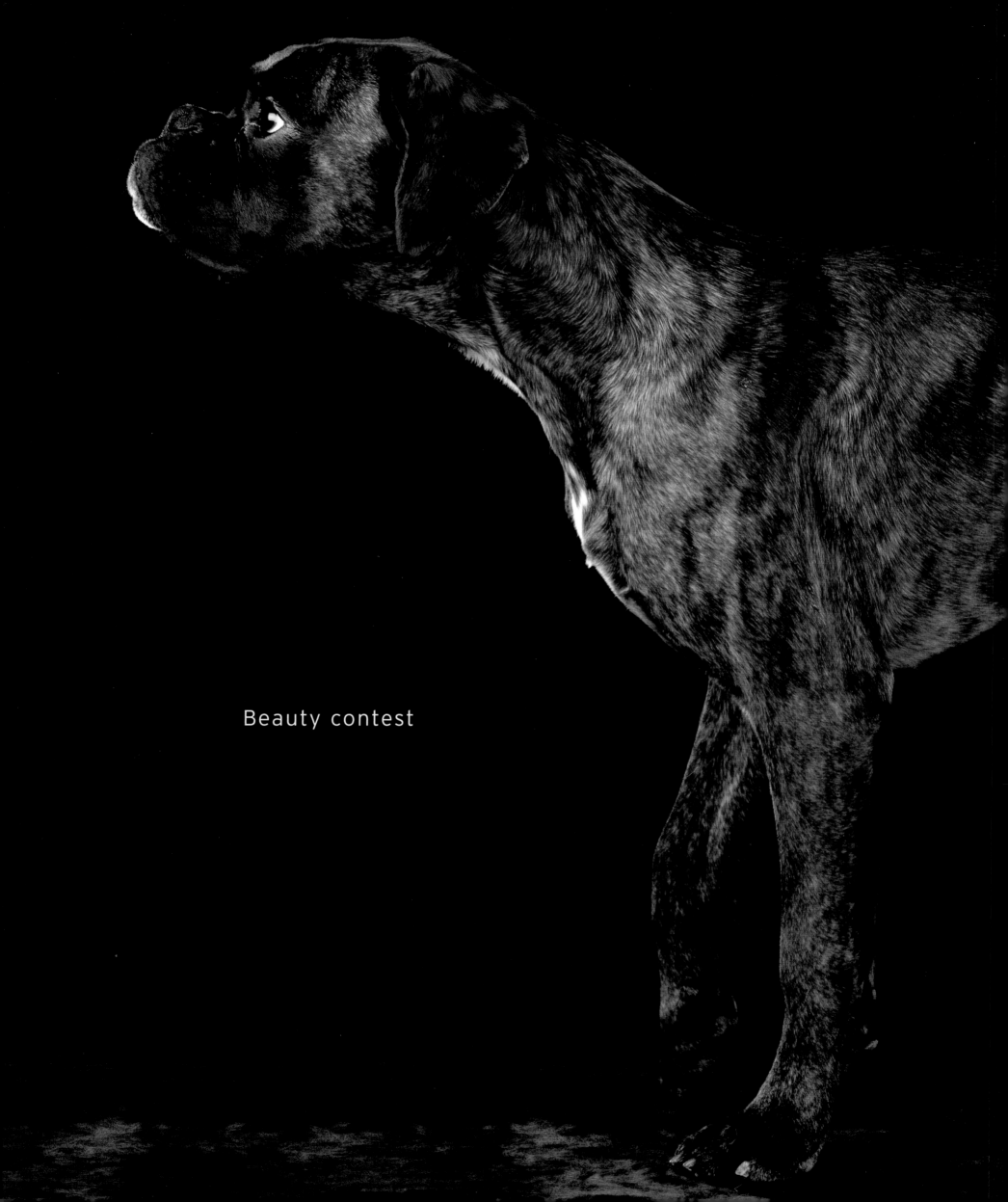

Beauty contest

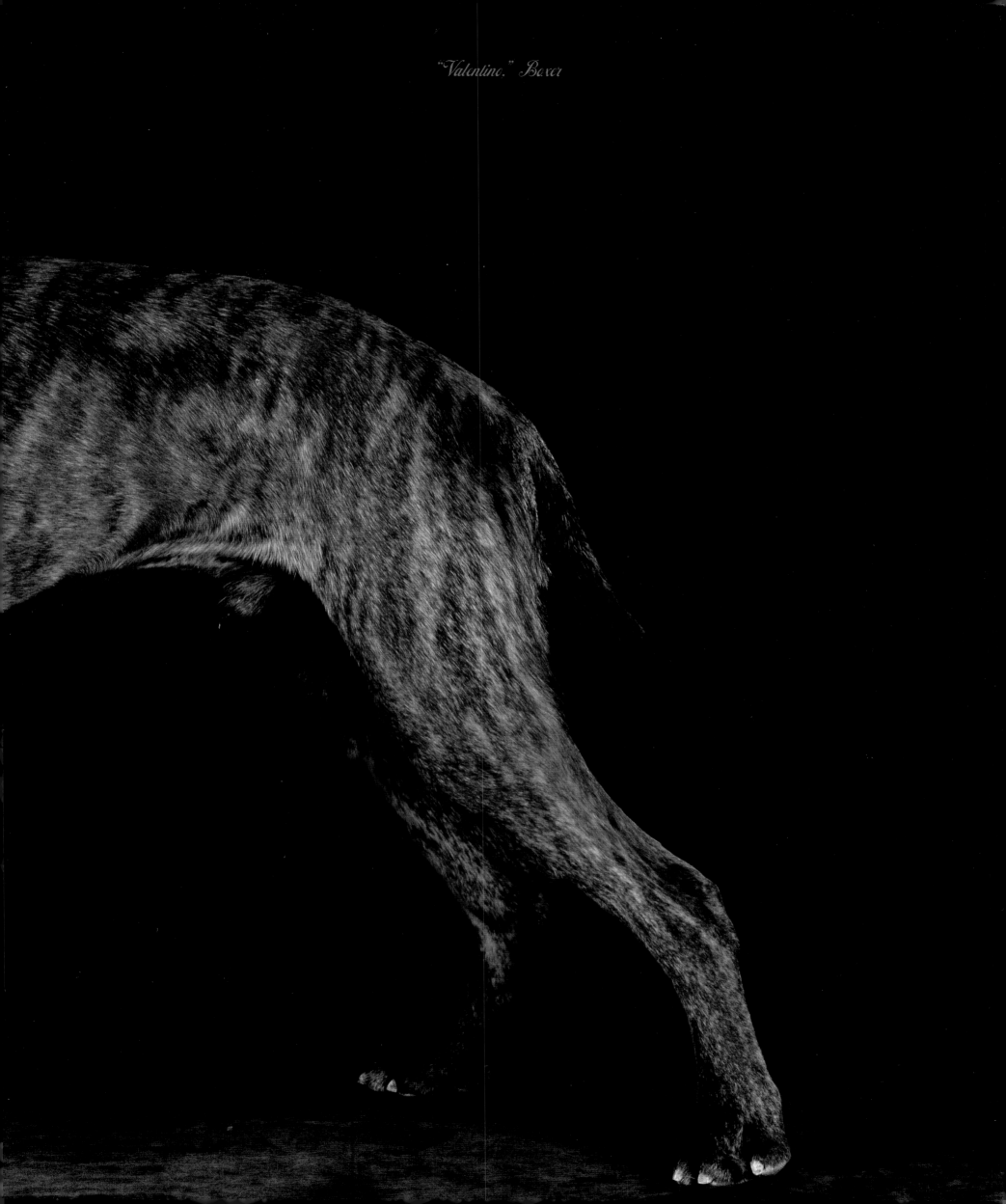

"Valentino." Boxer

LITTLE DOGS
GROWING UP

*"Cur di Salustri" and "Caught My Eye," Terranova and Labrador Retriever*

# Little lords of the manor . . .

with a desire to grow

Man chose the most childlike features of the wolf to obtain dogs. Nature then did the rest and highlighted dog's features in puppies, by multiplying wrinkles, carefreeness and awkwardness. This is how the basis of attraction was laid, which is the first step towards friendship. And that's how the dog became man's best friend.

*"Clementina," Jack Russell Terrier*

"Cesira," Bulldog

"Cesira" and "Ottavio," Bulldogs

"Denzel" English Setter

"Joker." German Shepherd

Mood swings

ON THE MARCH

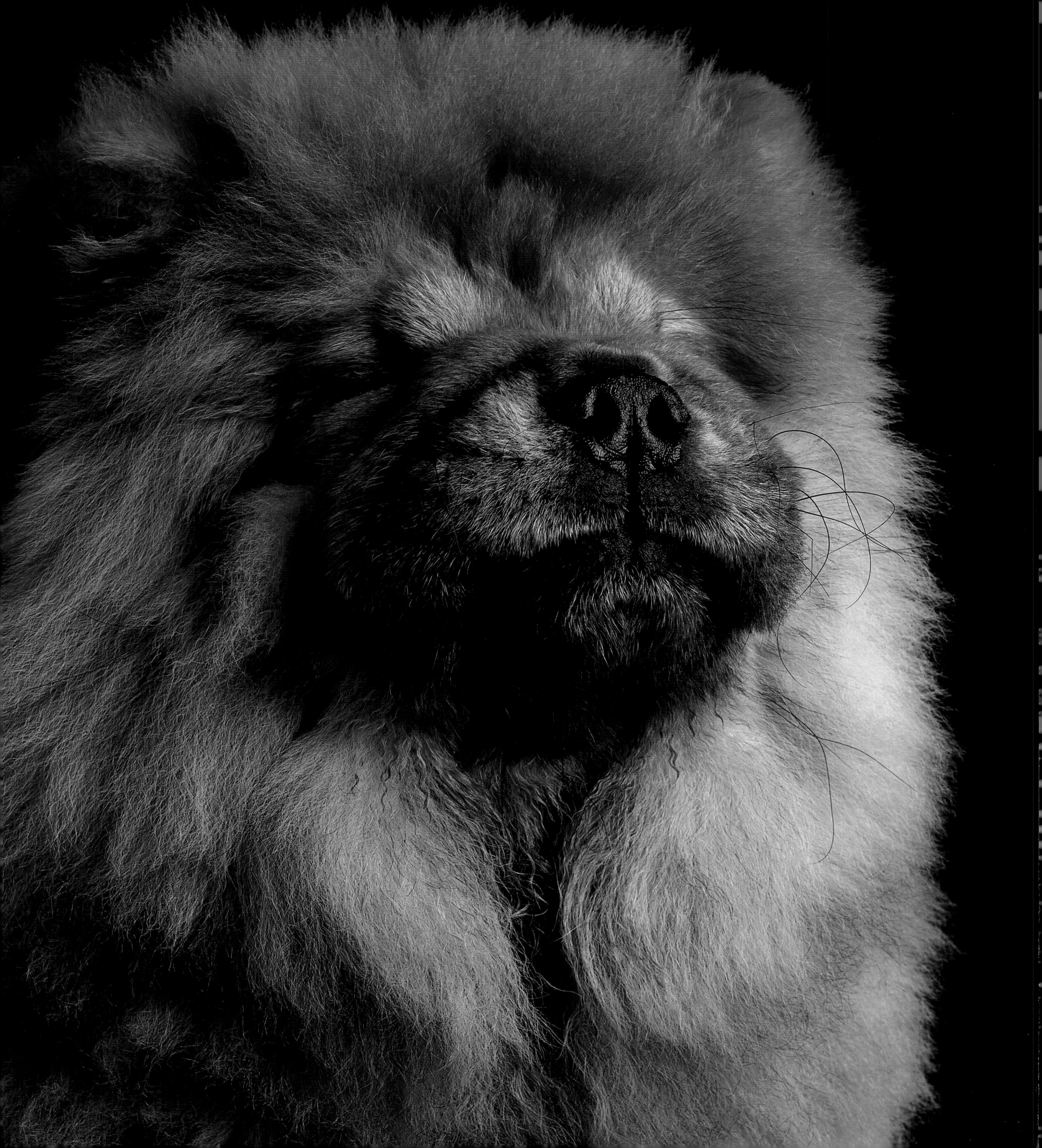

"Alastor Light Bringer," Chow Chow

Dog or lion?

# EXPRESSION WRINKLES

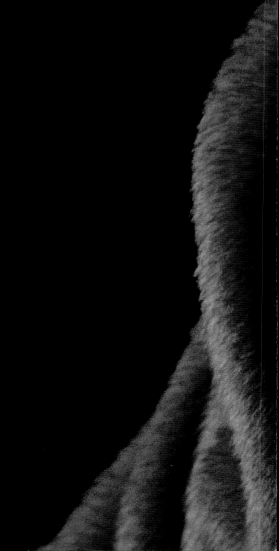

*"Oscar," Shar-Pei*

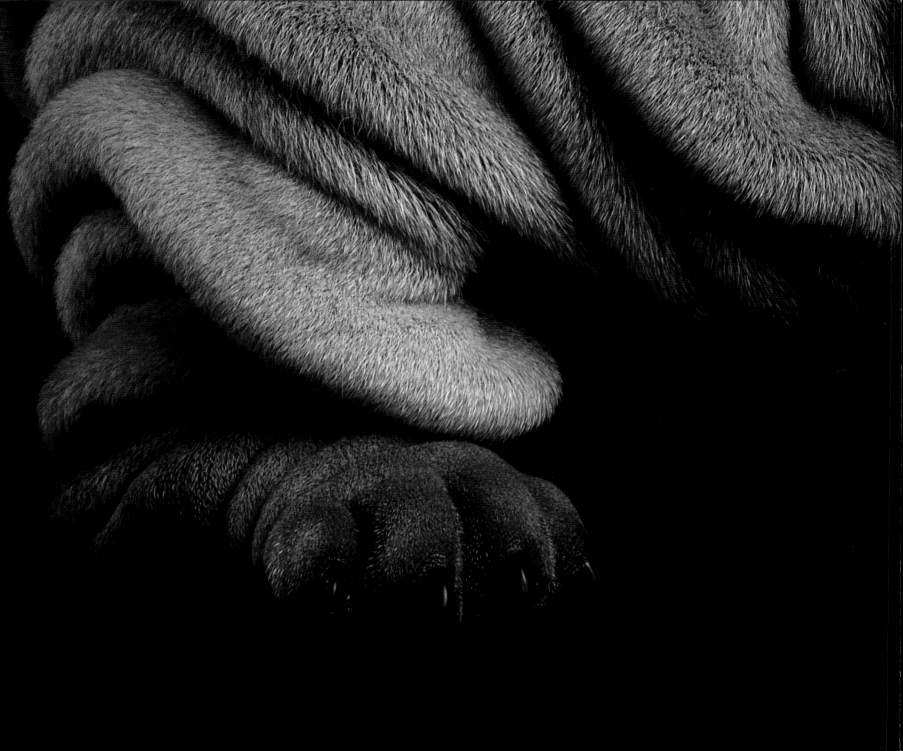

"Dogs often reflect the most hidden sides of one's character"
(Anonymous)

"Oscar," Shar-Pei

"Oscar." Shar-Pei

Different points of view

*"Codope di Plevan,"* Terranova

Two rascals

"No one appreciates
the very special genius
of your conversation
as the dog does"

(C. Morley)

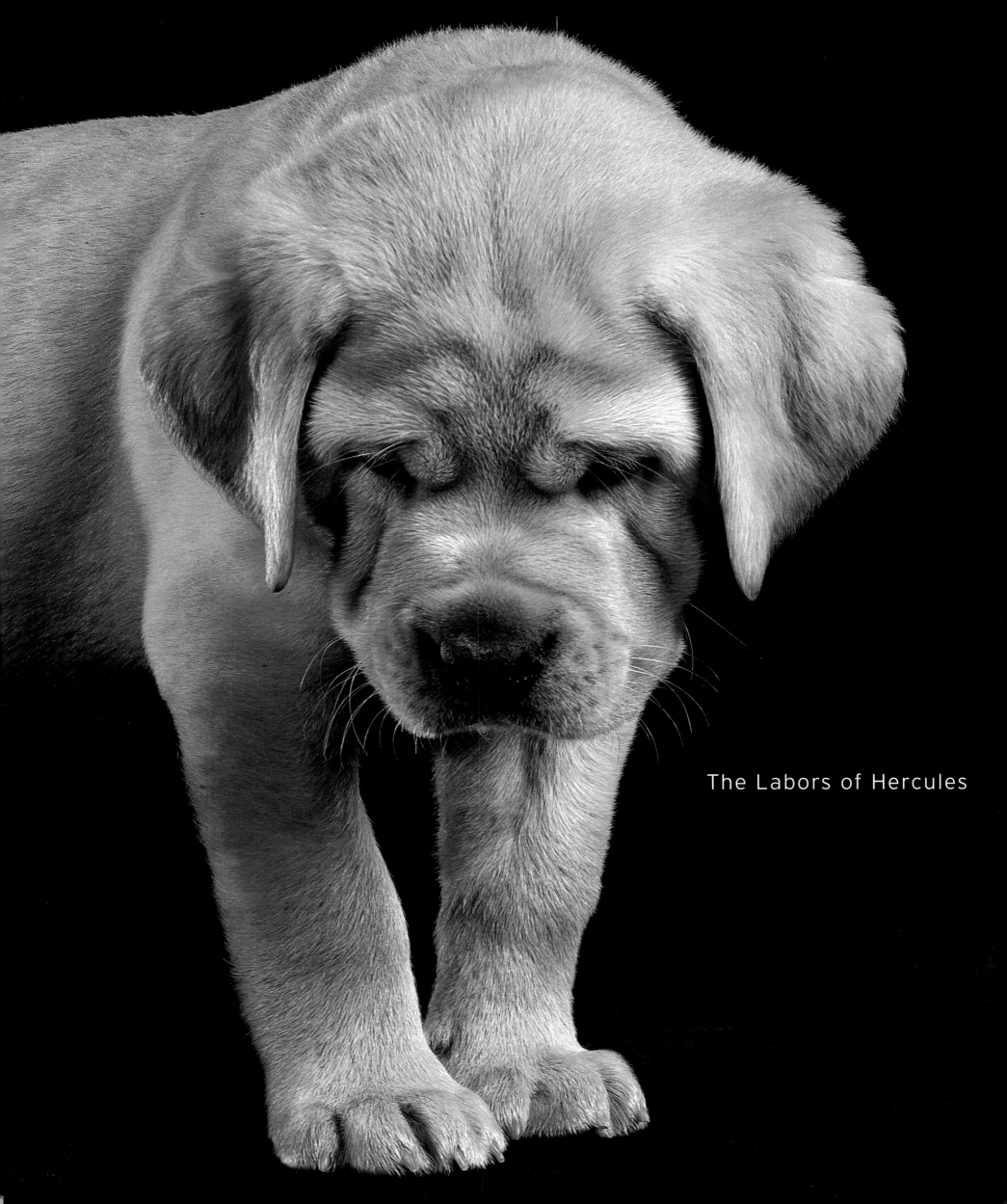

The Labors of Hercules

# YIN AND YANG

" No matter how little money
and how few possessions,
you own, having a dog
makes you rich "

(Louis Sabin)

Dog or wolf?

ON A BREAK

*"Chers Souvenirs," Bernese Mountain Dog*

"ten sheep . . . eleven sheep . . . twelve sheep . . ."

*"Ottavio." Bulldog*

"I'm not thinking about anything, anything at all . . ."
(Fernando Pessoa)

GENERATIONS FACE TO FACE

*"Denzel" and "Bannerun Dreamscape," English Setters*

# Big ones and little ones . . .

a never-ending race

**Maternal instinct shows itself in full force when puppies are defenseless, shapeless babies. But they better not ask for any comforting suckling once they reach two months of age: mother will not spoil them, will not cuddle them, but will only supervise. It is now man's turn, although most of the work has been done: the puppy is now a dog.**

Like father, like son

LESSONS IN LIFE

"Xanadu" and "Captain Hook." Labrador Retrievers

# FATHERLY PRIDE

"Rollo Mac Loud" and "Copy Cat," Labrador Retrievers

GIANT STEPS

# One paw after the other

*"Joker" and "Ramiro," German Shepherds*

"Heart to Heart" and "Cracklyn Fusion," Golden Retrievers

MODELS OF LIFE

Dialogue
between generations

"Madonna" and "Bonnie." Alaskan Malamutes

# HEAD TO HEAD

# Meaningful looks

Growing up tired

"Il Chel Famos" and "Cur di Salustri," Terranovas

"Clementina" puppy and "Fantasy" adult, Jack Russell Terriers

JUMPS,
JOKES
AND SNEERS

*"Dinni" and "Rosita," Bergamasco Sheephound and Wire-haired Dachshund*

# Jumps and expressions. . .

Whoever said dogs can't talk? What are those grimaces, those wags, those somersaults, those moves . . . if not words?

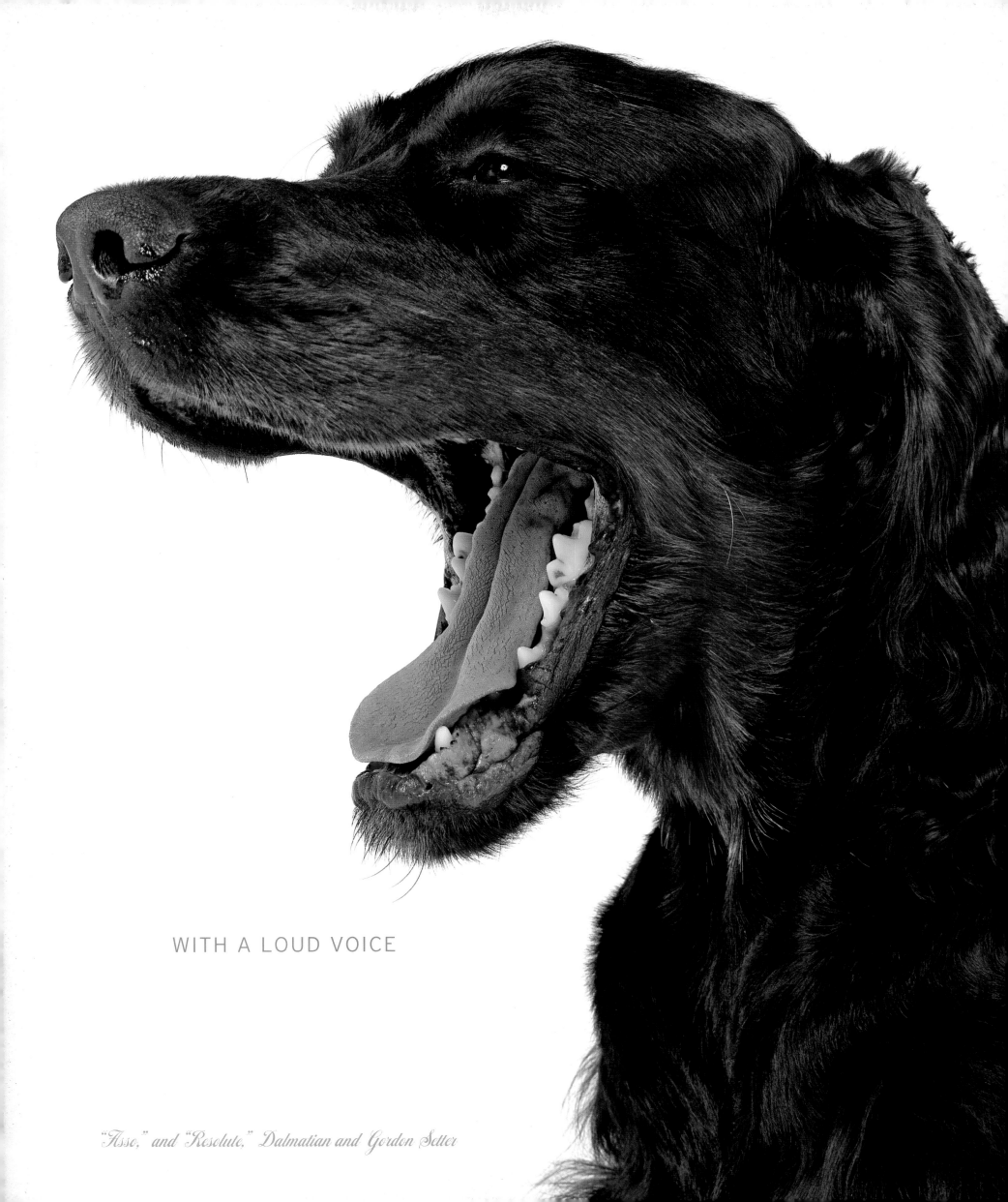

WITH A LOUD VOICE

"Asso," and "Resolute," Dalmatian and Gordon Setter

"Ustica" and "Eco," Boxers

ATHLETIC

MARTIAL ARTS

From dawn to dusk

*"Ithos" and "Holy," Bernese Mountain Dogs*

Anything for a pat

*"Holy," Bernese Mountain Dog*

*"Martino," Weimaraner*

ACROBATS

"Martino," Weimaraner

SLOW MOTION

"Zelig," Boxer

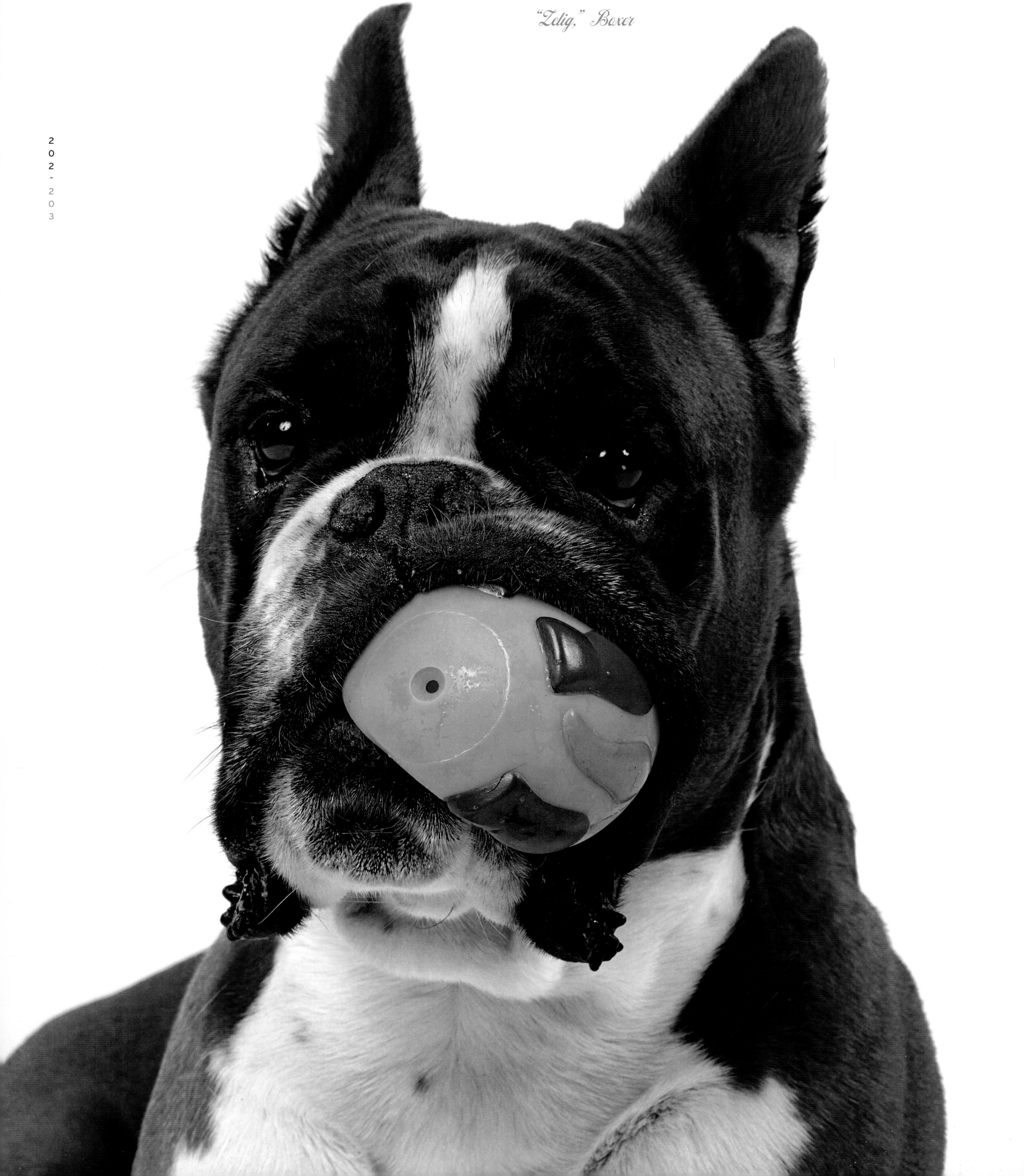

"The great pleasure of a dog is that you may make
a fool of yourself with him and not only will he not scold you,
but he will make a fool of himself too"

(Samuel Butler)

360°

*"Penelope," Boxer*

"Quarky," German Shepherd

Fred Astaire

"Cesarione," Bracco Italiano

A sportsman at heart

*"Bannerun Dreamscape," English Setter*

BATMAN

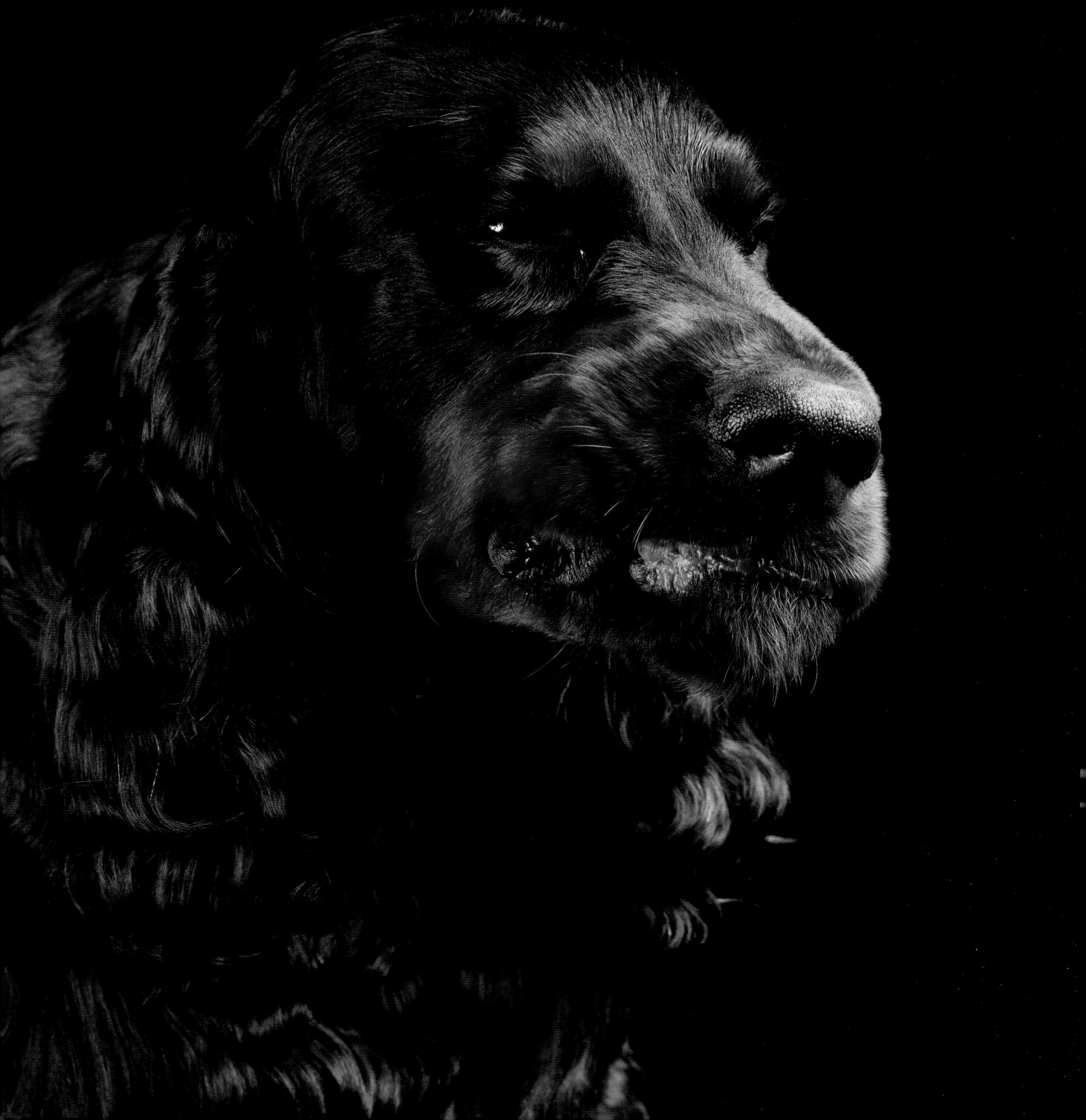

*"Resolute," Gordon Setter*

GRIMACES

DIABOLIK

*"Torquemada," Skye Terrier*

A great party

Guilty or innocent?

An irreverent character

When dogs yawn
they look like humans

"River," English Setter

"Eco," Boxer

FOCUSED

DISTRACTED

Tit-for-tat

"Argentina," Bouvier des Flandres

*"Sherbert Lemon," Petit Basset Griffon Vendeen*

"If a dog's wishes
came true, bones would
rain from the sky"
(Anonymous)

"Dinni," Bergamasco Sheepdog

Music maestro...

*"Ranzham," Clumber Spaniel*

# The Publisher would like to thank

**"ANTICA CALEDONIA" - E.N.C.I. - F.C.I. MEMBER**
**Breed:** Skye Terrier
Manager: Mrs. Laura Calistri
**Address:** Via di Valtriano, 50 - 56043 Valtriano (PI)
**Tel.:** cell. +39 340 3086846
**e-mail:** kennel@anticacaledonia.it
**Internet** www.anticacaledonia.it
Titles: International Ch.: 35 / Italian Ch.: 75 / French Ch.: 1 / E.N.C.I. Young Promises: 10 / World Ch.: 2 / Top Stud Ch.: 15 / Social Ch.: 25 / European Ch.: 5 / American Ch.: 3 / B.I.S.: 15

**"BASSA PAVESE" - E.N.C.I. - F.C.I. MEMBER**
**Breed:** Irish Wolfhound
Manager: Dr. Ludovica Salomon Ivaldi
**Address:** Via Cadorna, 24 - 27016 Sant'Alessio con Vialone (PV)
**Tel.:** +39 0382 953245 - cell. +39 335 309974
**e-mail:** ludovica@ludstar.it
**Internet** www.ludstar.it/bassapavese
Titles: World Ch.: 2 / European Ch.: 4 / International Ch.: 7 / Italian Ch.: 31 / Monaco Ch.: 6 / B.I.S.: countless

**"BEL PASTUR" - E.N.C.I. - F.C.I. MEMBER**
**Breed:** Briard
Manager: Mr. Franco Partegiani
**Address:** Via S. Angela Merici, 9 - 25032 Chiari (BS)
**Tel.:** +39 030 712765
**e-mail:** info@delbelpastur.com
**Internet** www.delbelpastur.com
Titles: Italian Ch.: 22 / French Ch.: 1 / E.N.C.I. Young Promises: 3 / Top Stud Ch.: 11 / European Junior Ch.: 1 / Russian Ch.: 1 / Canadian Ch.: 1 / American Ch.: 1 / Mediolanum Trophy: 2 / Roversi Trophy: 1 / Union Européenne du Berger de Brie Junior Ch.: 2 / Elite Stud Berger de Brie Association: 2 / Best of Breed at French Specialty: 2 / Selected Breed at French Specialty: 17 / Best of Breed at Canadian Specialty: 1

**"BIANCO ARANCIO" - E.N.C.I. - F.C.I. MEMBER**
**Breed:** English and Irish Setter
Manager: Dr. Maria Lisa Giuliani
**Address:** Via Americi, 690 - 47020 Cesena (FC)
**Tel.:** +39 0547 415685 - cell. +39 338 5099845
**e-mail:** info@biancoarancio.com
**Internet** www.biancoarancio.com
Titles: Italian Ch.: 12 / International Ch.: 12 / San Marino Ch.: 4 / World Ch.: 1 / Vice World Ch.: 1 / E.N.C.I. Young Promises: 7 / German Ch.: 1 / Luxembourgian Ch.: 1 / Top Dog of the Year: 2 / B.I.S.: 4 / R.B.I.S.: 3 Italian Working Dog trials Ch.: 1 / CAC: 3 / CACIT: 1

**"CASA BEGGIATO" - E.N.C.I. - F.C.I. MEMBER**
**Breed:** German Shepherd
Manager: Mr. Stefano Beggiato
**Address:** Via Calatafimi, 15 - 20052 Monza
**Tel.:** +39 039 2003538 - cell. +39 348 2202084
**e-mail:** info@casabeggiato.it
**Internet** www.casabeggiato.it
Titles: Many titles from the specialized society S.A.S. (Società Amatori Schaferhunde [Amateur Shepherd Society]) – "Speranze, Promesse e Auslesi." For working breeds : 1st place with Working Certificate and Endurance Trials. All breeds are sired by parents chosen according to morphological-character criteria, and have obtained results in Show and Work trials.

**"CASA CALBUCCI" - E.N.C.I. - F.C.I. MEMBER**
**Breed:** Beagle
Manager: Mr. Alberto Calbucci
**Address:** Strada Terrabianca, 1375 - 47025 Piavola (FC)
**Tel.:** +39 0547 694020 - cell. + 39 392 7935450
**e-mail:** info@dicasacalbucci.it
**Internet** www.dicasacalbucci.it
Titles: Italian Ch.: 20 / E.N.C.I. Young Promises: 10 / a few International, Breeders' and Social Championships in Monaco, San Marino, Slovenian, Croatian / B.I.S.: 1
Work trials: C.A.C., or other reserves and qualifications: about 50 on hare tracking/ Breeders' Trophy, 2003, 2004 and 2005.

**"DELOR DE FERRABOUC" - E.N.C.I. - F.C.I. MEMBER**
**Breed:** Bracco Italiano
Manager: Mrs. Lucia De Ferrabouc
**Address:** Via Ravellino, 5 - 20015 Parabiago (MI)
**Tel.:** +39 0331 556787 - cell. +39 335 6147559
**e-mail:** info@delorkennel.com
**Internet** www.delorkennel.com
Titles: Italian Ch.: 5 / Swiss Ch.: 2 / Austrian Ch.: 4 / German Ch.: 1 / E.N.C.I. Young Promises: 6 / Absolute Ch.: 10 / European Ch.: 3 / Hungarian Ch.: 1 / Polish Ch.: 1

**"DRAGONJOY" - E.N.C.I. - F.C.I. MEMBER**
**Breed:** Pembroke Welsh Corgi
Manager: Chiara Ceredi and Marcello Farnedi
**Address:** Via Cervese, 1101 - 47023 Cesena (FC)
**Tel.:** +39 0547 382504/384709
**e-mail:** chiaraceredi@alice.it
**Internet** www.dragonjoycorgis.com
Titles: Italian Ch.: 8 / International Ch.: 7 / European Ch.: 5 / San Marino Ch.: 6 / E.N.C.I. Young Promises: 7 / 2 Ch. for each country: English, Russian, Luxembourgian, Croatian, Slovenian, Monégasque / 1 Ch. for each country: Spanish, Czech Republic, Hungarian, Bosnia-Herzegovina, Poland / Winner Cajelli Trophy 2007: 1 / Top Pembroke Corgi 2007 in England: 1 / B.I.S.: 17 - R.B.I.S.: 11

**"DUNVEGAN" – E.N.C.I. MEMBER**
**Breed:** Labrador Retriever (page 168)
Manager: Mrs. Luciana Trivellone Perasso
**Address:** Loc. Rigaiolo, 78 - 53048 Sinalunga (Siena)
**Tel.:** +39 0577 678151 - cell. +39 347 7110055
**e-mail:** dunveganlabradors@virgilio.it
Titles: Italian Ch.: 1 / E.N.C.I. Young Promises: 1 / European Ch.: 1 (Veteran Class) / World Ch.: 1 (Veteran Class) / Europapokal Innsbruck: 1 - Tirreno Ch. 2002: 1 - Top Stud Ch.: 1 / B.I.S.: 1

**"GRANDI GRIGI" - AFFISSO E.N.C.I.**
**Breed:** Short-haired Weimaraner
Manager: Mrs. Silvia Fanetti
**Address:** Via delle Vignacce, 14/C - 52100 Arezzo
**Tel.:** cell. +39 339 1611422
**e-mail:** info@weimaranerdog.it
**Internet** www.weimaranerdog.it - www.deigrandigrigi.it
Titles: Italian Ch.: 3 / Austrian Ch.: 2 / San Marino Ch.: 3 / San Marino Ch. Junior: 1 / Croatian Ch. : 1 / Montecarlo Youth Ch.: 1 / E.N.C.I. Young Promises: 4 / Absolute Ch.: 1 / International Beauty Ch.: 1 / Young European Ch.: 1 / Crufts 2008: 2 / World Dog Show, Youth: 3rd absolute / Podiums at the B.I.S.: Breeder Couples: 16 / Breeder Groups: 8 / 7th Group (pointing dogs): 6

**"IULIUS" - E.N.C.I. - F.C.I. MEMBER**
**Breed:** Airedale Terrier and Soft-Coated Wheaten Terrier
Manager: Dr. Giulio Audisio di Somma
**Address:** Piazza Caduti, 9 - 10090 Trana (TO)
**Tel.:** +39 011-9338238 - cell. +39 338-2595424
**e-mail:** audisiodisomma@libero.it
**Internet** www.iuliusterriers.it
Titles: European Ch.: 7 / International Ch.: 15 / Italian Ch.: 27 / E.N.C.I. Young Promises: 10 / Top Stud Ch.: 5 / Social Ch.: 10 / San Marino Ch.: 8 / 3 Ch. for each country: Luxembourg and Slovenia / 2 Ch. for each country: Austria, Switzerland, Israel / 1 Ch. for each country: French, Russia, Monaco-Monte Carlo, Croatia, Bosnia, Ukraine, Lithuania, Estonia, Belorussia / Top Dog (Italia): 6 - Top Dog (French): 1 / Winner INTERRA: 8 / Al pelage Ch.: 1 / Alpidelmare Ch.: 1 / AlpeAdria Ch.: 3 / Baden Sieger: 3 / Bodensee Sieger: 2 / Bundessieger Austria: 1 / Winner St. Gallen: 5 / Club Champion Slovenian: 1 / Swiss Club Champion: 1 / Club Champion Russo: 1 / Club Champion Luxembourg: 2 / Trophy Mediolanum: 1 / Provincia Granda Trophy: 2 / T.A.N. (Natural Aptitude Test): 7

**"KHAMBALIQ" - E.N.C.I. - F.C.I. MEMBER**
**Breed:** Shar-Pei - Basset Hound
Manager: Mrs. Isabella Pizzamiglio
**Address:** Via Murillo, 27 - 04010 Sezze Stazione (LT)
**Tel.:** +39 0773 899269 - cell. +39 339 3132194
**e-mail:** info@sharpei-khambaliq.com
**Internet** www.sharpei-khambaliq.com
Titles: Italian Ch.: 67 / Swiss Ch.: 1 / German Ch.: 1 / E.N.C.I. Young Promises: 36 / Greek Ch.: 2 / American Ch.: 4 / South African Ch.: 5 / Peruvian Ch.: 2 / Spanish Ch.: 1 / Monaco Ch.: 4 / Luxembourgian Ch.: 1 / Gibraltar Ch. : 2 / Romanian Ch.: 2 / Bulgarian Ch.: 2 / B.I.S.: 1

**"LA GALDA"**
**Breed:** Bovaro delle Fiandre
Manager: Mr. Giovanni Fugazza
**Address:** Via Papa Giovanni XXIII, 24 - 26019 Vailate (CR)
**Tel.:** +39 0363 340015 - cell. +39 347 2953689
**e-mail:** info@lagalda.com
**Internet** www.lagalda.com
Titles: Italian Ch.: 4 / International Ch.: 3 / I.P.O.3: 2 / I.P.O.2: 2

**"LAGO DEGLI ORSI" - E.N.C.I. - F.C.I. MEMBER**
**Breed:** Alaskan Malamute - Basenji - Shiba Inu
Manager: Mrs. Gloria Urbani
**Address:** Via Gorgnona, 12/2 - 16146 Genova (GE)
**Tel.:** +39 010 908981 - +39 010 3629836
**e-mail:** info@lagodegliorsi.com
**Internet** www.lagodegliorsi.com
Titles: World Ch.: 14 / International Ch.: 46 / European Ch.: 14 / American Ch.: 20 / Canadian Ch.: 5 / San Marino Ch.: 5 / Croatian Ch.: 5 / Austrian Ch.: 6 / Slovakian Ch.: 6 / Hungarian Ch.: 4 / Slovenian Ch.: 4 / Czech Ch.: 4 / 3 Ch. for each country: Luxembourg, Finland, French / 2 Ch. for each country: Spain, Portugal, Poland / Bundessieger Ch.: 9 / 1 Ch. for each country: Germany, Sweden, Slovakia, Denmark, Holland, Greece, Estonia, Lithuania, Serbia, Mexico, Chile / VDH Ch.: 1 / Grand Slovakian Ch.: 1 / Eurocap Winner: 1 / Winner Copenhagen: 1 / Winner Helsinki: 2 / Young European Promise: 2 / Italian Year Champion: 2.
Work results: Award of Merit: 1 / Register of Merit: 3 / Working Weight Pull Italian Ch.: 45 / E.N.C.I. Young Promises: 14 / Social Ch.: 33 / Top Stud Ch.: 24 / dog: 2 / Working Team dog: 4 / Advanced Standard Agility: 6

**"LISANDER" - E.N.C.I. - F.C.I. MEMBER**
**Breed:** Black Russian Terrier
Manager: Mr. Marco Galli
**Address:** Via E. De Amicis, 4 - 25034 Orzinuovi (BS)
**Tel.:** +39 030 941355 - cell. +39 348 9117180
**e-mail:** marco@lisander.info
**Internet** www.lisander.info
Titles: Italian Ch.: 26 / International Ch.: 11 / European Ch.: 2 / World Ch.: 3 / E.N.C.I. Young Promises: 7 / Austrian Ch.: 3 / Russian Ch.: 2 / Ch. Absolute: 1 / Top Stud Ch.: 5 / Social Ch. Black Terriers: 5 / Winner E.N.C.I. Breeders Trophy 2007 / B.I.S.: 3

**"LUDSTAR" - F.C.I. - E.N.C.I. MEMBER**
**Breed:** Gordon Setter
Manager: Dr. Michele Ivaldi
**Address:** Via Cadorna, 24 - 27016 Sant'Alessio con Vialone (PV)
**Tel.:** +39 0382 953245 - cell. +39 333 2720711
**e-mail:** Michele@ludstar.it
**Internet** www.ludstar.it
Titles: World Ch.: 15 / International Ch.: 15 / European Ch.: 9 / Italian Ch.: 25 / French Ch.: 1 / German Ch.: 4 / Spanish Ch.: 4 / English Ch.: 2 / American Ch.: 1 / Monaco Ch.: 7 / E.N.C.I. Young Promises: 1 / Ch. Absolute: 1 / International Absolute Ch.: 1 / Beauty Ch.: 33 / BOB Crufts 2003 and 2006 / BOS Crufts 2008

**"DELLA MAGA" - E.N.C.I. - F.C.I. MEMBER**
**Breed:** Boxer and smooth-haired Dachshund Standard
Manager: Mrs. Monica Feri
**Address:** Via della Greve, 14 - 50124 Firenze (FI)
**Tel.:** +39 055 2048671 - cell. +39 339 1243169
**e-mail:** dellamaga@libero.it
**Internet** www.dellamaga.it
Titles: Italian Ch.: many / Austrian Ch.: 5 / German Ch.: 4 / Ch. Absolute: 2 / World Ch.: 2 / European Juniors Ch.: 2 / B.I.S.: 2
Work results: Selections: 20 / CAL 3: countless

**"NICONICO" - E.N.C.I. - F.C.I. MEMBER**
**Breed:** Cairn Terrier and Norfolk Terrier
Manager: Mr. Nico Danovaro
**Address:** Viale Cambiaso, 3 - 16145 Genova (GE)
**Tel.:** +39 010 381605 - cell. +39 339 7320363
**e-mail:** info@norfolkterrier.it
**Internet** www.norfolkterrier.it
Titles: Italian Ch.: 8 / E.N.C.I. Young Promises: 7 / International Ch.: 9 / Slovenian Ch.: 5 / Croatian Ch.: 5 / Club Winner: 4 / E.N.C.I. 2005 Champions

**"ROYAL CREST GOLD-N" - E.N.C.I. - F.C.I. MEMBER**
**Breed:** Golden Retriever
Manager: Mr. Colorado Fiorentini
**Address:** Strada Vicinale Barborini - Tabiano, Salsomaggiore (PR)
**Tel.:** cell. +39 335 5903071
**e-mail:** royalcrestgoldn@tiscali.it
**Internet** www.royalcrestgoldn.it
Titles: Absolute Ch.: 4 / Vice-World Ch.: 2 / World Youth Ch.: 2 / Social Ch.: 15 / Italian Ch., English, French, International, Monégasque, Swiss, Austrian, Croatian, Montenegrin, Sammarinese: other 100 titles. / B.I.S. : Royal Crest U.S.A. Direct Champion, the only Golden Retriever in the history of Italian dog breeding to win Best in Show in International Dog Show.
Work results: CAC: 25 / CACIT: 6 / Challenge Benelli-Top Retriever: 8

**"SAORE" - E.N.C.I. - F.C.I. MEMBER**
**Breed:** Scottish Terrier and Sealyham Terrier
Manager: Mrs. Antonella Maggiori
**Address:** Via Ciserano, 11 - Osio di Sotto (BG)
**Tel.:** +39 035 4823625
**e-mail:** antonella@saore.com
**Internet** www.saore.com
Titles: Italian Ch.: 16 / E.N.C.I. Young Promises: 1 / International Ch.: 6 / American Ch.: 1 / Swedish Ch.: 3 / Social Ch.: 7 / T.A.N. (Natural Aptitude Tests) 3 / B.I.S.: 2 - R.B.I.S.: 1 / Terrier of the Millennium: 1 / Winner Amsterdam: 1 / Top Dog: 3

**"STARRY TOWN" - E.N.C.I. - F.C.I. MEMBER**
**Breed:** Terranova and Bernese Mountain Dog
Manager: Mr. Maurizio Mauro
**Address:** Via Carletti, 3 - 33050 Campolonghetto (UD)
**Tel.:** +39 0432 996433 - cell. +39 348 8017205
**e-mail:** info@starrytown.it
**Internet** www.starrytown.eu
Titles: World Ch.: 1 / European Ch.: 2 / International Ch.: 15 / Italian Ch.: 10 / Austrian Ch.: 5 / American Ch.: 2 / Canadian Ch.: 2 / Peruvian Ch.: 2 / Serbia-Montenegro Ch.: 5 / Bosnia-Herzegovina Ch.: 2 / E.N.C.I. Young Promises: 3 / 1 Ch. for each country: French, Portugal, Norway, Sweden, Finland, Estonia-Lithuania, Greece. / Social Ch.: 1 / Mediterranean Ch.: 1 / Nordic Ch.: 1 / B.I.S.: 20

**"TINTAGEL WINDS" - F.C.I. - S.C.C. MEMBER**
**Breed:** Labrador Retriever
Manager: Felicity and Kira Leith-Ross
**Address:** Felicity: 722 route de Prailles - 74140 Sciez s/Leman – FRANCE
Kira : Skelton - Saltburn by the sea - Cleveland - ENGLAND
**Tel.:** France +33 450948681 - cell. +33 615350016
England: +44 1287659574 - cell. +44 7854110514
**e-mail:** TWlabradors@twlabradors.com
**Internet** www.twlabradors.com
Titles: French Ch.: 17 / Swiss Ch.: 14 / Italian Ch.: 2 / Belgian Ch: 6 / English Ch.: 1 / European Ch.: 2 / World Ch.: 1 / International Ch.: 31 / Other National Championships: 36
Work results: Field Trial Ch.: 7 - Trialers Ch. (French): 33

**"TOUCHSTAR" - E.N.C.I. - F.C.I. MEMBER**
**Breed:** Jack Russell Terrier
Manager: Mrs. Francesca Scorza
**Address:** Via Cadorna, 22 - 27016 Sant'Alessio con Vialone (PV)
**Tel.:** cell. +39 347 4975104 - cell. +39 338 1384957
**e-mail:** info@jackrussell.it
**Internet** www.jackrussell.it
Titles: Italian Ch.: 10 / Swiss Ch.: 4 / Austrian Ch.: 2 / German Ch.: 1 / E.N.C.I. Young Promises: 14 / World Ch.: 4 / Social Ch.: 7 / European Ch.: 3 / Danish Ch.: 2 / Swedish Ch.: 2 / - B.I.S.: 2 - R.B.I.S.: 4

**"VADO RECUPERO E TORNO" - E.N.C.I. - F.C.I MEMBER**
**Breed:** Cocker Spaniel and Clumber Spaniel
Manager: Mrs. Liana Pacco
**Address:** Via Casabianca, 3/A - 33041 Aiello del Friuli (UD)
**Tel.:** cell. +39 349 8709443
**e-mail:** paccoliana@tiscali.it
**internet** www.cocker-clumber.it
Titles: Italian Ch.: 1 / Slovenian Ch.: 1 / Monaco Ch.: 1 / Croatian Ch.: 1 / San Marino Youth Ch.: 1 / B.I.S.: 4

**"VENTO CELESTE" - E.N.C.I. - F.C.I. MEMBER**
**Breed:** Chow Chow
Manager: Mrs. Emma Cosenza Poggi
**Address:** Via di Valle Bianchella, 9 - 00060 Sacrofano (RM)
**Tel.:** +39 06 9086703 - cell. +39 339 6407565
**e-mail:** emmacose@tin.it - info@allevamentodelvento.com
**internet** www.allevamentodelvento.com
Titles: Italian Ch.: 3 / E.N.C.I. Young Promises: 2 / Social Ch.: 1 / International Ch.: 1 / San Marino Ch.: 2 / San Marino Youth Ch.: 6

**"VURRIAVASÀ" – BECOMING E.N.C.I. MEMBER**
**Breed:** Bulldog and Dachshund
Manager: Mrs. Daniela Natalini de Pompeis
**Address:** Strada Signorino snc – 01100 Viterbo (VT)
**Tel.:** +39 0761 307503 - cell. +39 333 4790990 - cell. +39 328 3051938
**e-mail:** info@britishbulldod.it
**internet** www.britishbulldog.it
Titles: I have been breeding Bulldogs for almost 20 years. I adore bringing up my pups but I do not like taking part in exhibitions if not the bare minimum to simply verify the typicality of my breeds. Puppies are home-bred, I pay great attention to socialization. My adult dogs live in the family and not in kennels, and selection is based on three fundamental requisites: lack of pathologies (especially genetic ones); character: I think it is necessary that the dog has balance, sociability, affection towards its entire family, as well as lack of aggressiveness. These qualities make a well selected bulldog a unique dog; typicality: the attempt to feature physical characteristics the closest possible to the breed standard.

**"YOGHI'S SEAL" - E.N.C.I. - F.C.I. MEMBER**
**Breed:** Cairn Terrier
Manager: Mrs. Paola Dall'Anese
**Address:** C.so Umberto I, 161 - 13031 Arborio (VC)
**Tel.:** +39 0161 869103 - 0161 866015 - cell. +39 329 3037764
**e-mail:** dallanesepaola@libero.it
Titles: Italian Ch.: 3 / E.N.C.I. Young Promises: 3 / Top Stud Ch.: 1 / Social Ch.: 2

**AMATEUR SCHNAUZER BREEDER MR. ROCCA FULVIO**
**Breed:** Schnauzer
Proprietario: Mr. Giorgio Del Prete
**Address:** Loc. Chiusura, 63 - 52024 S. Giustino Valdarno (AR)
**Tel.:** +39 055 9866863 - cell. +39 055 977328
Titles: International Ch.: 1 / Italian Ch.: 1 / E.N.C.I. Young promises: 1 / Social Ch. Youth: 1 / Social Ch. Free: 1 / Promises World Champions Camp. 2000 Milan: 1

© 2008 White Star S.p.A.
Via Candido Sassone, 22/24
13100 Vercelli, Italy
www.whitestar.it

Translation: Marco Visentin

ISBN 978-88-544-0331-4

Reprints:
1 2 3 4 5 6   12 11 10 09 08

Color separation Chiaroscuro, Turin and Fotomec, Turin
Printed in Indonesia

**The Publisher would like to thank**
Nanni Trivellone and Luciana Perasso for their collaboration, Mr. Nicola Maisto, the Salvadori family, owners of the Agricola Senese in Sinalunga
and Mr. Artigiani from Telemondo in Calcinaia for the shoot locations.


**The Author would like to thank**
Matteo Barale who, in addition to lending his assistance during the long period of the photo campaign,
assembling the photo set and organizing the lights, contributed to a successful job by entertaining
400 dogs with patience and dedication.

Special thanks to Rita Paesani, who worked with the author on the first three photo shoots.